Ronald Duncan, who died before he had completed his work on this collection, was renowned as an author, poet and playwright. The book was completed by Melvin Harris, well known as a BBC radio presenter, especially of his researches into the widest possible range of subjects, from the social history of music and musical instruments to that of all kinds of scientific invention.

Gray Jolliffe's work appears regularly in newspapers and magazines and he has won many advertising awards, both as a copy writer and as an artist.

# CRITICS' GAFFES

RONALD DUNCAN
WITH MELVIN HARRIS

Futura
Macdonald & Co
London & Sydney

A Futura Book

First published in Great Britain in 1983 by
Macdonald & Co (Publishers) Ltd
London & Sydney

This Futura edition published in 1984

ISBN 0 7088 2568 0

Printed in Great Britain by Collins.

Futura Publications
A Division of
Macdonald & Co (Publishers) Ltd
Maxwell House
74 Worship Street
London EC2A 2EN
A BPCC plc Company

# CONTENTS

# ACKNOWLEDGEMENTS

Ronald Duncan wished to acknowledge the help he received in compiling this book from Professor Sir Hermann Bondi, FRS, Profesor E.W.F. Tomlin, Professor Ray Lyttleton, FRS, Colin Wilson and Mr Andrew Lawson. His Estate wishes to acknowledge Melvin Harris's work in completing it.

# AUTHORS, POETS & PLAYWRIGHTS

## J.M. BARRIE
*Peter Pan*

Oh, for an hour of Herod!

> Anthony Hope, after the first night.

## CHARLES BAUDELAIRE
*Fleurs du Mal*

… the collection contains … not one poem which is plain and can be understood without a certain effort – an effort seldom rewarded, for the feelings which the poet transmits are evil and very low ones. And these feelings are always, and purposely, expressed by him with eccentricity and lack of clearness.

> Leo Tolstoy, *What is Art*

## SAMUEL BECKETT
*Waiting for Godot*, first performed 1956

*Waiting for Godot* … is another of those plays that tries to lift superficiality to significance through obscurity. It should please those who prefer to have their cliches masquerading as epigrams.

> Milton Schulman

I've been brooding in my bath, and it is my considered opinion that the success of *Waiting for Godot* is the end of the theatre as we know it.

> Robert Morley

## LIONEL BRITTON
*Brain*

His ability to deliver anything is not clear to me. My belief is that Mr Shaw was so stunned by his inability to understand a word of it that he concluded it must be brilliant ... Cracked I call it.

> St John Erving, after reading
> George Bernard Shaw's review.


## GEORGE GORDON, LORD BYRON

We counsel him to forthwith abandon poetry ... and whatever judgement may be passed on the poems, it seems we must take them as we find them and be content, for they are the last we shall ever have from him. He is at his best an intruder in the groves of Parnassus.

> *Edinburgh Review*


He makes virtue serve as a foil to vices ... the noble lord is almost the only writer who has prostituted his talents in this way.

> William Hazlitt


*Don Juan*

Don Juan ... cannot be read by persons of moral and religious feelings without the most decided reprobation.

> *London Magazine*

## THOMAS CARLYLE

Carlyle is like pickles; only a little of him can be tasted, with any relish, at a time.

Anon.

We shall regard it as one of the most melancholy evidences of the decline of all pure and healthful literature, if the writings of Mr Carlyle continue to have an enduring hold upon the popular mind.

*Church of England Quarterly Review*

## MARC CONNELLY
*Green Pastures* (1930)

... dreadfully lacking in box-office appeal.

*Variety* (New York) February, 1930.


## JOSEPH CONRAD

I cannot abide Conrad's souvenir-shop style, bottled ships and shell necklaces of romantic cliches.

Vladimir Nabokov

# CHARLES DICKENS

It would take a heart of stone not to laugh aloud at the death of
Little Nell.

Oscar Wilde

No popularity can disguise the fact that this is the very lowest of low styles of art.

> Sir James Fitzjames Stephen, 1859

*Our Mutual Friend* is, to our perception, the poorest of Mr Dickens' works. And it is poor with the poverty not of momentary embarrassment, but of permanent exhaustion. It is wanting in inspiration. For the last ten years it has seemed to us that Mr Dickens has been unmistakeably forcing himself. *Bleak House* was forced; *Little Dorrit* was laboured; the present work is dug out as with a spade and pickaxe.

> Henry James, 1865

Thought is strangely absent from his works. I do not suppose a single thoughtful remark on life or character could be found throughout the twenty volumes.

> George Henry Lewis, 1872

Mentally drowned and blinded by the sticky overflowings of his heart, Dickens was incapable, when moved, of re-casting, in terms of art, the reality which had moved him, was even, it would seem, unable to perceive that reality.

> Aldous Huxley, 1930

It is because Dickens' characters have no mental life ... Dickens is able to reach simple people, which Tolstoy is not.

> George Orwell, 1940

BENJAMIN DISRAELI, later LORD BEACONSFIELD
*Coningsby*

The fashionable novel, pushed … to its extremist verge, beyond which all is naught. It is a glorification of dandyism, far beyond all other glories which dandyism has attained.

William Makepeace Thackeray

JOHN DONNE

Were he translated into numbers, and English, he would yet be wanting in the dignity of expression.

John Dryden

The poetry consists of heterogeneous ideas yanked by violence together.

Dr Samuel Johnson

Donne's studied roughness of meter has the hesitancy and the thoughtfulness of speech; even at its most musical his poetry is that of a man speaking.

Graham Greene

T.S. ELIOT
*Essays*

… his inability to communicate the pleasure he has derived from literature and his refusal to reveal … the mysteries he himself had penetrated become, in the end, an irritation, an offence …. though he writes of poetry, he is coldly detached from it and although life is the stuff of literature, we cannot feel that he has ever lived.

Gerald Cumberland, *Written in Friendship*

*The Lovesong of Alfred J. Prufrock*

A drunken helot … The reduction to absurdity of literary licence.

Arthur Waugh

*The Waste Land*

Fanciful patchwork of parodies and learned borrowings.

Anon.

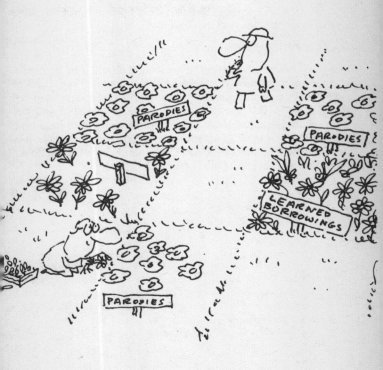

A farrago of nonsense.

> Clement Wood, 'The Tower of Drivel'
> in *Call Magazine* (New York), June 1923

Unintelligible, the borrowings cheap and the notes useless.
> F.L. Lucas, *The New Statesman and Nation*, November 1923

A grunt would serve equally well.
> J.C. Squire, *The London Mercury*, October 1923

## ANATOLE FRANCE

I should describe him as first class second class. To be great as a writer one must have originality, and also a certain nobleness of mind ... he was by nature selfish, and mean to the verge of sordidness ... The French both in literature and in other walks of life, when they have not a great man they pretend to have one. Towards the end of Anatole's life everybody of real weight had disappeared, so that he stood alone, challenging attention in his splendid and successful mediocrity.

> W.B. Maxwell, *Time Gathered*

## ROGER FRY

What, I ask you is Roger Fry? – a literary gentleman, or a painter? My God, look at his pictures! The pen is mightier than the palette in his case.

D.H. Lawrence

## THOMAS HARDY
*Jude*

When I finished the story I opened the windows and let in the fresh air, and I turned to my bookshelves and said: 'Thank God for Kipling and Stevenson, Barrie and Mrs Humphry Ward'.

Anonymous American critic

Swinburne planteth, Hardy watereth and Satan giveth increase.
Anonymous Scottish critic

The village aesthetics brooding over the village idiot.
G.K. Chesterton (1914)

The gloom is not even relieved by a little elegance of diction.
Lytton Strachey (1914)

**W.H. HUDSON**
*The Purple Land*

We feel bound to say that we have seldom been called upon to express an opinion on a more vulgar farrago of repulsive nonsense.

*Saturday Review*, September 1885


**HENRIK IBSEN**
*The Master Builder*

Rather 'The Master Bewilderer'!

Israel Zangwill


*Ghosts*

Realism is one thing; but the nostrils of the audience must not be visibly held, before a play can be stamped as true to nature.

Leader in the *Daily Telegraph*, 14 March 1891


**HENRY JAMES**

... an idiot, and a Boston idiot to boot, than which there is nothing lower in the world ...

H.L. Mencken


... he piled up sentence after sentence and parenthetic side issues – till at last all was obscurity, and obscurity he thought was cleared when he discovered the elusive word he wanted. This was what his style became in his books.

Stopford Brooke

Having first made sure that he has scarcely anything left to express, he then sets to work to express it ... He spares no resource in the telling of his dead inventions ... He brings up every device of language to state and define ... His vast paragraphs sweat and struggle ... And all for tales of nothingness ... It is a magnificent but painful hippopotamus resolved at any cost, even at the cost of its dignity, upon picking up a pea which has got into a corner of its den.

H.G. Wells

## DR SAMUEL JOHNSON

I own I like not Johnson's turgid style,
That gives an inch the importance of a mile;
Casts of manure a wagon-load around,
To raise a simple daisy from the ground;
Uplifts the club of Hercules – for what?
To crush a butterfly, or brain a gnat.

'Peter Pindar' (Dr John Wolcot)

… insolent and loud,
vain idol of a scribbling crowd …
… who, proudly seized of learning's throne,
now damns all learning but his own.

Charles Churchill

# JAMES JOYCE

... Joyce is rather inaudible, because he is talking to himself ...

G.K. Chesterton

My God, what a clumsy *olla putrida* James Joyce is! Nothing but old fags and cabbage stumps of quotations from the bible and the rest, stewed in the juice of deliberate, journalistic dirty-mindedness – what old and hard-working staleness, masquerading as the all-new!

D.H. Lawrence

In Ireland they try to make a cat clean by rubbing its nose in its own filth. Mr Joyce has tried the same treatment on the human subject. I hope it may prove successful.

George Bernard Shaw

## Finnegans Wake

Joyce talked to himself in his sleep: hence *Finnegans Wake*.

Oliver Gogarty

## Ulysses

My considered opinion, after long reflection, is that whilst in many places the effect of *Ulysses* on the reader undoubtedly is somewhat emetic, nowhere does it tend to be an aphrodisiac. *Ulysses* may, therefore, be admitted to the United States.

John M. Woolsey, U.S. District Judge

## JOHN KEATS

The impressible nature of Keats would naturally incline him to erotic composition, but his early love-verses are remarkably deficient in beauty and even in passion. Some which remain in manuscript are without any interest, and those published in the little volume of 1817 are the worst pieces in it.

Lord Houghton, *Life and Letters of John Keats* (1840)

To ascertain the merit of a poem is one thing: to determine the powers of a poet, is another. The present paper aims at the latter. Such being the case, the faults of Keats' poetry may be divided in two classes: 1. those of youth and inexperience; 2. those of deficiency of genius. Out of the former he might (had his life been spared) have grown: the latter he would have kept till his death-bed.

*Cambridge University Magazine*, March 1840

## JACK KEROUAC

That's not writing. that's typing.

Truman Capote

## RUDYARD KIPLING

A lady who writes fiction reveals her sex clearer through her portrayal of men than through any other of her lapses ... In Kipling's short stories ... men are portrayed ... from an essentially feminine point of view.

Max Beerbohm

## D.H. LAWRENCE

Filth. Nothing but obscenities.

Joseph Conrad

Lawrence's contempt for the world accumulated within his mind until finally he could announce it only in thin, strident shrieks.... one must draw the line somewhere. And the object of a line through Lawrence – if, indeed, the line is flexible enough not to exclude him altogether – must be to divide the sane from the insane.

Norman Collins, *The Facts of Fiction*

SINCLAIR LEWIS
*Arrowsmith*

As a mind Martin Arrowsmith suffers from arrested development, as a scientist he is a *fool* ... Is not the same true of Mr Lewis' characters in general?... The lives explored are uncomplicated, the experience revealed is mediocre ... The critics have never been sure whether Mr Lewis was trying to truly represent the life of his time or to caricature it, and it seems likely that Mr Lewis has shared their uncertainty.

Bernard DeVoto, *The Literary Fallacy*


*Hobohemia*

The author's strategy consists in the very simple process of representing the citizens of this burg as howling idiots, and the Mid-Western young lover as a paragon of brainy, homely virtue. It is a stand-off between the two lots as to which is the more preposterous ... The most successful feature of the production is its title.

John Corbin, *New York Times*

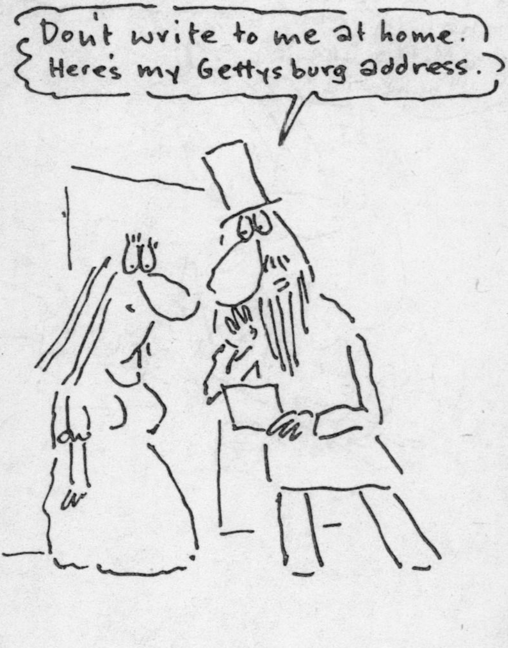
Don't write to me at home. Here's my Gettysburg address.

## ABRAHAM LINCOLN
*The Gettysburg Address*

The President acted without sense ... so let us pass over his silly remarks.

*The Patriot*, Harrisburg

The cheek of every American must tingle with shame as he reads the silly, flat utterances of the President.

*The Chicago Times*

Anything more dull and commonplace it would not be easy to produce.

*The Times*, London

## HENRY WADSWORTH LONGFELLOW
*Hiawatha*

We cannot but express a regret that our own pet national poet should not have selected as the theme of his muse something higher and better than the silly legends of the savage aborigines.

*Boston Globe*

## NORMAN MAILER
*The Naked and the Dead*

It's a fake. A clever, talented, admirably executed fake.

Gore Vidal

## HERMAN MELVILLE
*Moby Dick*

He knows nothing of the sea. Fantastic – ridiculous.

Joseph Conrad

He has indulged himself in a trick of metaphysical and morbid meditations … he has succeeded in vitiating both his thought and style with an appearance of the widest affectation and untruth.

Fitz-James O'Brien, *Putnam's Magazine*, 1857

## HENRY MILLER
*Tropic of Cancer*

From first to last page a filthy, cynical, disgusting narrative of sordid amours. Not only is there in it no word or suggestion of the romantic, sentimental, poetic or spiritual aspects of the sex relation, but it is not even bawdy sex, or comic sex, or sex described with good humour. No glory, no beauty, no stars – just mud …

Chief Justice Desmond

## A.A. MILNE

I see no future for Mr A.A. Milne, whose plots are as thin as a filleted anchovy, and whose construction is reminiscent of Victorian fret-work. It seems to me that Mr Milne is obsessed by the bogey of impossible stage-butlers who would be sacked directly they opened their mouths in real life. He conceives a fragment, splits it and pads it in cotton-wool through three acts, but so far he has not conceived one idea of value.

H. Dennis Bradley (1925)

## WILLIAM MORRIS
*The Defence of Guenevere*

To our taste, the style is as bad as bad can be. Mr Morris imitates little save faults. He combines the mawkish simplicity of the Cockney school with the prosaic baldness of the worst passages of Tennyson, and the occasional obscurity and affectation of plainness that characterize Browning and his followers.

*Spectator*, February 1858

... all that he produces – pictures of queer, quaint knights, very stiff and cumbrous, apparently living all day in chain armour, and crackling about in cloth of gold – women always in miniver, and never in flesh and blood.

*Saturday Review*, November 1858

C.G.-B

VLADIMIR NABOKOV
*Lolita*

I am afraid that I have been horrified and appalled by the thought that you might publish it....the physical details, both in lascivious description and by implication are ... disgusting ... As to its literary value ... I can see none ... how greatly I should deplore your firm publishing this book ... it will tarnish the bright name of Weidenfeld and Nicolson.

Victoria Sackville-West to Nigel Nicolson, December 1958

BORIS PASTERNAK

... a pig who dirties the place where he sleeps and eats, and who dirties those he lives with and by whose labours he exists.

V. Semichastny

The petty, cowardly, mean and philistine character of Dr Zhivago, who is as alien to the Soviet people as is the malignant literary snob Pasternak.

*Literaturnaya Gazeta*

Don't fret Boris. They'll change their tune when they see the movie!
DR ZHIVAGO
'RUBBISH'

## LUIGI PIRANDELLO

A funny fellow
Whose curious plays
Enjoyed a craze,
And ran for *days*!

Reginald Arkell

## EDGAR ALLAN POE

There comes Poe, with his raven, like Barnaby Rudge
Three fifths of him genius and two fifths sheer fudge.

James Russell Lowell, 'A Fable for Critics'

## EZRA POUND

I must confess I cannot enjoy Pound's poetry ... [He] seems to me
a poet of few natural gifts.

Cyril Connolly

I could never regard him as a poet and have consistently denied
him the title.

Robert Graves, letter to T.S. Eliot

*Provença* (*Personae & Exultations* in US edition)

We began the examination of this book of poems with great
expectations and we lay it down with considerable contempt for
the bulk of English criticism that has pretended to discover in
these erratic utterances the voice of a poet.

'WSB', *Boston Evening Transcript*, December 1910

*The Ballad of The Goodly Fere*

Mr Pound has made the fishermen of Galilee into north-country
sailors of the Patrick Spens tradition and given them sentiments
more proper to the left wing of the YMCA.

Laura Riding and Robert Graves,<br>*Survey of Modernist Poetry* (1927)

*Cantos*

*The Cantos* appear to be little more than a game – a game
serious with the seriousness of pedantry. We may recognize what
Mr Pound's counters stand for, but they remain counters; and his
patterns are not very interesting, even as schematic design, since,
in the nature of the game, which hasn't much in the way of rules
(without reference to a philosophy or to any teleological
principles) they lack definition and salience.

*Hound and Horn*, Winter 1931

## MARCEL PROUST

To [his] first volume he has added a second one which prolongs the first, and he is preparing two more on the same theme. There is nothing to prove that he will stop going on his merry way. In my opinion, only fatigue or death can stop him in the task he has undertaken of searching for his lost time.

'Gasquet', contemporary French review

## WILLIAM SHAKESPEARE

*Hamlet*

Hamlet is nothing more than the maudlin introspection of a bourgeois.

Kenneth Tynan

*Twelfth Night*

*Twelfth Night* is but a silly play.

Samuel Pepys

*The Sonnets*

If Shakespeare had written nothing but his sonnets … he would … have been assigned to the class of cold, artificial writers, who had no genuine sense of nature or passion.

William Hazlitt

The sonnets beginning CXXVII to his mistress are worse than a puzzle-peg. They are abominably harsh, obscure, and worthless. The others are for the most part much better…. Their chief faults – and heavy ones they are – are sameness, tediousness, quaintness, and elaborate obscurity.

William Wordsworth

Not a single one is very admirable … They are hot and pothery: there is much condensation, little delicacy, like a raspberry jam without cream, without crust, without bread, to break its viscidity.

Walter Savage Landor

## GEORGE BERNARD SHAW
*Heartbreak House*

We can expect little more in modern comedy from Mr Bernard Shaw. Twenty years ago he was ten years ahead of his time; now the world has grown up and past him. *Heartbreak House* has broken his spell and we have tired of his mechanical women who never lived.

H. Dennis Bradley (1925)


## ALAN SILLITOE
*Saturday Night and Sunday Morning*

I still think that Mr Sillitoe, on the evidence of this film, has little to say except that a good wage, accessible sex, and a telly aren't everything. Any Sunday-school teacher could have made the point in fewer words.

'Majdalany', *Daily Mail*, October 1960


## ROBERT LOUIS STEVENSON

He imagined no human soul and he invented no story that anyone will remember.

George Moore, *Daily Chronicle*, April 1897


The great work he is to write by-and-by when the little works are finished ... He experiments too long; he is still a boy wondering what he is going to be ... It is quite time the great work was begun.

J.M. Barrie

## DYLAN THOMAS
*Under Milk Wood*

... the embodiments have no moral existences, and there is no conflict, development, or synthesis: everything is equally of amusing interest, as to a child, and this lack of essential drama makes *Under Milk Wood* a tedious piece of verbal 'ingenuity', redeemed only by its innuendoes and salacious jokes.

David Holbrook, *Pelican Guide to English Literature*

I saw and heard his *Under Milk Wood* on television, and I thought that the best thing in the programme was the 20-minute breakdown ... I regarded it, and the characters who appeared in it, with repulsion ... It seemed to me that the man who wrote it had a mind like a sewer. There were few people in this fictional place whose thoughts did not dwell most of the time on booze or lechery or both. I do not believe that any Welsh village, or any village, is inhabited by so many unpleasant people. I therefore conclude that Dylan Thomas must have been an exceptionally unpleasant person.

George Murray, *Daily Mail*, May 1957

## PAUL VERLAINE
*Ariettes*

How does the moon seem to live and die in a copper heaven? And how can snow shine like sand? The whole thing is not merely unintelligible, but, under pretence of conveying an impression, it passes off a string of incorrect comparisons and words

Leo Tolstoy, *What is Art?*

## EVELYN WAUGH
*Black Mischief*

Whether Mr Waugh still considers himself a Catholic, the *Tablet* does not know; but, in case he is so regarded by booksellers, librarians, and novel-readers in general, we hereby state that his latest novel would be a disgrace to anybody professing the Catholic name. We refuse to print its title or to mention its publishers.

Ernest Oldmeadow, *Tablet*, January 1933

This 'Book of the Month' dated from Stonyhurst and signed by an author whose conversion had been widely and loudly bruited, turned out to be a work both disgraceful and scandalous. It abounds in coarse and sometimes disgusting passages, and its climax is nauseating.

Ibid., February 1933

## OSCAR WILDE

As a dramatist, novelist and poet, he was very loyally imitative; except for his last comedy, all his plays, though laced with glittering veins of wit, are commonplace in thought and structure.

> Peter Quennell, *A History of English Literature*

Neither in literature nor in life was tragedy his natural element. His role was not to plumb the depth of feeling, but flicker delicately across the surface.

> Ibid.

*An Ideal Husband*

... so helpless, so crude, so bad, so clumsy, feeble and vulgar.

> Henry James

## THORNTON WILDER
*The Skin of Our Teeth*

It is a strange performance that Mr Wilder has turned in ... Is he hoaxing us? On the one hand he gives no credit to his source, masking it with an Olsen and Johnson technique. On the other hand, he makes no attempt to conceal his borrowings, emphasizing them rather, sometimes even stressing details which with a minimum of ingenuity he could have suppressed or altered.

> *Saturday Review of Literature*, December 1942

## ANGUS WILSON
*The Wrong Set*

We end by being repelled and by feeling that it is not quite decent to enjoy so much ugliness and humiliation. There ought to be some noble value somewhere ... But the things worth saving in *The Wrong Set* have been degraded almost beyond recognition ...

Edmund Wilson, *New Yorker*, April 1950

## COLIN WILSON
*The Outsider*

The book itself is inaccurate in detail and fraudulent in method to the point of being very bad. The reason these things were not detected by the reviewers is that it said what they wanted to hear ...

Martin Green

## W.B. YEATS

... those 'bee-loud-glade' verses of W.B. Yeats that with their sweet poison have ruined half the Irish verse of the last two decades.

Gerald Cumberland, *Written in Friendship*

## ÉMILE ZOLA
*Rougon-Macquart's Saga*, on publication of final volume

If I were to write ... it would be to advise Zola, now that the family-tree of the Rougon-Macquarts is complete, to go and hang himself from the highest branch.

Alphonse Daudet

# COMPOSERS, CONDUCTORS & MUSICIANS

## JOHANN SEBASTIAN BACH

... kills the feeling for pure melody, and awakes the delight in ingenious contrapuntal combinations for which any idea, even the most trivial, will serve, although it expresses nothing and has not the least melodic charm.

Johann Christian Lobe (1797-1881)

... from an artistic point of view I put little value upon the logical demonstrations in sound worked out by John Sebastian Bach. I do not consider them, from a musical point of view, to be any superior to the mathematical demonstrations made by a good professor at any European university.

W.J. Turner, *Musical Times*, December 1932

# LUDVIG VAN BEETHOVEN

Beethoven always sounds to me like the upsetting of bags of nails, with here and there an also dropped hammer.

John Ruskin

... this extraordinary genius was completely deaf for nearly the last ten years of his life, during which his compositions have partaken of the most incomprehensible wildness. His imagination seems to have fed upon the ruins of his sensitive organs.

William Gardiner, *The Music of Nature* (1837)

Beethoven took a disliking to uneuphonious dissonances because his hearing was limited and confused. Accumulations of notes of the most monstrous kind sounded in his head as acceptable and well balanced combinations.

A. Oublicheff, *Beethoven, ses critiques et ses glossateurs* (1857)

*Fidelio* (revised version, 1806)

Recently there was given the overture to Beethoven's opera Fidelio, and all impartial musicians and music lovers were in perfect agreement that never was anything as incoherent, shrill, chaotic and ear-splitting produced in music.

August von Kotzebue, *Der Freimutige* (Vienna), September 1806

*Concerto for Violin and Orchestra*

Beethoven's concerto for violin and orchestra (op. 61) ... was longer and more tedious still. I have not a single good word for it. If the subject of the last movement was the tune of one of Arthur Robert's comic songs, or any music-hall song, it would do very nicely and I daresay we should often hum it. I do not mean at the opening of the movement but about half way through, where the character is just that of a common music-hall song and, so far, so good.

Samuel Butler

*Third Symphony, 'Eroica'*

The inordinate length of this ... wearies even the cognoscenti and is unendurable to the mere music lover ... if Beethoven continues on his present path both he and the public will be the sufferers.

Anonymous nineteenth-century critic

*Sixth Symphony, 'Pastoral'*

Opinions are much divided concerning the merits of the *Pastoral Symphony* of Beethoven, though very few venture to deny that it is much too long.

*The Harmonicon* (London), June 1823

*Seventh Symphony*

... Beethoven's Seventh Symphony ... is a composition in which the author has indulged a great deal of disagreeable eccentricity. Often as we now have heard it performed, we cannot yet discover any design in it, neither can we trace any connection in its parts. Although it seems to have been intended as a kind of enigma – we had almost said a hoax...

Ibid., July 1825

*Eighth Symphony*

Beethoven's Eighth Symphony depends wholly on its last movement for what applause it obtains; the rest is eccentric without being amusing, and laborious without effect.

Ibid., June 1827

*Ninth Symphony*

We find Beethoven's Ninth Symphony to be precisely one hour and five minutes long; a fearful period indeed, which puts the muscles and lungs of the band, and the patience of the audience to a severe trial ...

Ibid., April 1825

... not only do I not see how the feelings transmitted by this work could unite people not specially trained to submit themselves to its complex hypnotism, but I am unable to imagine to myself a crowd of normal people who could understand anything of this long, confused, and artificial production, except short snatches which are lost in a sea of what is incomprehensible. And therefore, whether I like it or not, I am compelled to conclude that this work belongs to the rank of bad art.

Leo Tolstoy, *What Is Art?*

## VINCENZO BELLINI
*La Sonnambula* (Covent Garden Revival, 1910)

Rarely can an opera quite so supremely ridiculous … have been put upon the stage. The childishness of the plot, and the sheer inanity of the music combine, indeed, to give it a right to the title of the silliest opera in the world – and yet we tolerate it at the beginning of the twentieth century.

*Globe*

… many of the women wore diamond necklaces, not one had a tiara. What is Covent Garden on a Tetrazzini or Melba night without tiaras? This may seem a trivial observation, but really a musical critic cannot be expected to listen seriously to Bellini's poor music. It is so dull, and there is really nothing for the soprano to sing until the last Act.

*Daily News*

There is undoubted power in the closing scene, but one has to yawn through three acts of tedious action and melodious nothing to get to it.

*Observer*

There are surely few works whose soporific qualities are greater. As a cure for insomnia it should prove invaluable. What strikes one always about these old Italian works, which are supposed to be so full of melody, is their extraordinary poverty in this very particular. There are melodies of a kind, but they are all so tame and characterless that they go for little or nothing.

*Westminster Gazette*

## HECTOR BERLIOZ

This is the way Berlioz composes – he splutters the ink over the pages of ruled paper and the result is as chance wills it.

Frédéric Chopin

... rather class him as a daring lunatic than a sound, healthy musician ... we feel inclined to believe M. Berlioz utterly incapable of producing a complete phrase of any kind. When, on rare occasions, some glimpse of a tune makes its appearance, it is cut off at the edges and twisted about in so unusual and unnatural a fashion as to give one the idea of a mangled and mutilated body.... the little tune that seems to exist ... is of so decidedly vulgar a character as to exclude the possibility of our supposing him possessed of a shadow of feeling.

J.W. Davidson, *Musical Examiner*, 1843

One must draw the line somewhere, and the writer would draw it on the hitherside of such movements as the 'Orgies', which form the finales of *La Symphonie Fantastique* and *Harold en Italie*, or the chorus of devils in the *Damnation de Faust*. Bloodthirsty delirious passion, such as is here depicted, may have been excited by gladiator and wild beast shows in Roman arenas: but its rites ... reflected through the medium of music, are assuredly more honoured in the breach than the observance.

Edward Dannreuther, *Grove's Dictionary of Music* (1879)

What a good thing it isn't music.

Gioacchino Rossini

His scoring is so messy and slapdash that you want to wash your hands after going through one of his works.

Felix Mendelssohn

## GERALD HUGH TYRWHITT-WILSON, LORD BERNERS

… not a giant … a rather small and certainly impertinent man (I am writing of Lord Berners as a composer, of course).… the great bludgeon with which he hacked his way … was but a child's toy hammer.

Gerald Cumberland, *Written in Friendship*

## ALEXANDER BORODIN
*Symphony in B Minor*

We have no desire to hear Borodin's masterpiece again. Twice we suffered it, and failed to see any trace of greatness in music that not once takes us anywhere near 'the Edge of the Infinite' … or even faintly suggests an inspiration.

*Musical Times*, March 1898

## JOHANNES BRAHMS

Yesterday we studied the new symphony of Brahms – a composer who is praised to the Heavens in Germany … In my opinion he is dark, cold and full of pretence, of obscurity without true depth. I think Germany is on the decline musically …

Peter Tchaikovsky

*Motets for Double Chorus* (First British performance, 1891)

I will not deny that there was a sort of broken thread of vocal tone running through the sound-fabric; but, for the most part, it was a horrible tissue of puffing and blowing and wheezing and groan-, ing and buzzing and hissing and gargling and shrieking and spluttering and grunting and generally making every sort of noise that is incidental to bad singing, severe exertion, and mortal fear of losing one's place. It was really worse than influenza.

George Bernard Shaw, *The World*

*Symphony in E Minor*

The art of composing without ideas has most decidedly found in Brahms its worthiest representative.

Hugo Wolf


*Requiem*

There are some sacrifices which should not be demanded twice from any man, and one of them is listening to Brahms' *Requiem*.

George Bernard Shaw


BENJAMIN BRITTEN
*The Rape of Lucretia*

In fact, there were moments when one longed for the excellent little orchestra to go out and have a drink so that we could hear the words.

Beverley Baxter MP, *Evening Standard*, July 1946


When, in *The Rape*, Britten has three people singing different words with Lucretia in bed it sounds like bedlam to me. I can only sigh with relief when the band drowns the lot.

Preston Benson, *Star*, August, 1946


One cannot finish with Lucretia's death. I think that the present pseudo- religious ending came as an afterthougt. It is appalling, of course; but to ask for a simple surgical operation is quite senseless. A proper alternative would require a re-writing of the whole opera ... Everywhere Mr Britten reminds us of his favourite composers ...

William Glock, *Time and Tide*, October 1946

# FRÉDÉRIC CHOPIN

The entire works of Chopin present a motley surface of ranting hyperbole and excruciating cacophony … When he is not thus singular, he is no better than Strauss or any other waltz compounder … There is an excuse at present for Chopin's delinquencies; he is entrammelled in the enthralling bonds of that arch-enchantress, George Sand, celebrated equally for the number and excellence of her romances and her lovers; not less we wonder how she, who once swayed the heart of the sublime and terrible religious democrat Lammenais, can be content to wanton away her dreamlike existence with an artistical nonentity like Chopin.

*Musical World*, October 1841

Chopin was essentially a drawing-room composer. Away from his nocturnes and mazurkas he became as trivial and incoherent as in those attractive trifles he was earnest and individual.

*The Times*, May 1855

### Concerto in E Minor

… for the most part a rambling series of passages, with one or two pretty motivi, with which but little is done.

Ibid.

### The Mazurkas

Had he submitted this music to a teacher, the latter, it is to be hoped, would have torn it up and thrown it at his feet – and this is what we symbolically wish to do.

L. Rellstab, *Iris*, July 1833

*Nocturne in E Flat*

Where John Field smiles Chopin makes a grinning grimace; where Field sighs Chopin groans; where Field shrugs his shoulders Chopin twists his whole body; where Field puts some seasoning into the food Chopin empties a handful of cayenne pepper.

Ibid.

*Tarantella*, Opus 43

Nobody can call that music.

Robert Schumann

CLAUDE DEBUSSY
*L'Après-midi d'un faune*

Debussy's *L'Après-midi d'un faune* was a strong example of modern ugliness. The faun must have had a terrible afternoon, for the poor beast brayed on muted horns and whinnied on flutes, and avoided all trace of soothing melody, until the audience began to share his sorrows.

Louis Elson, *Boston Daily Advertiser*, February 1904

## La Mer

It is possible that Debussy did not intend to call it *La Mer* but, *Le Mal de Mer*, which would at once make the tone-pictures as clear as day. It is a series of symphonic pictures of sea-sickness. The first movement is 'Headache'. The second is 'Doubt', picturing moments of dread suspense, whether or no! The third movement, with its explosions and rumblings, has now a self-evident purpose. The hero is endeavouring to throw up his boot-heels!

*Boston Daily Advertiser*, March 1907

*The Sea* is persistently ugly.... it is prosaic in its reiteration of inert formulas ... Debussy fails to give any impression of the sea ... There is more of barnyard cackle in it than anything else.

*New York Times*, March 1907

## Pelléas et Mélisande

Rhythm, melody, tonality, these are three things unknown to Monsieur Debussy and deliberately disdained by him. His music is vague, floating, without colour and without shape, without movement and without life.

Arthur Pougin, *Le Menestrel*, May 1902

... there is nothing in it – no music. It has nothing consecutive – no musical phrases – no development ... I am a musician and I hear nothing.

Richard Strauss

## FREDERICK DELIUS
*Piano Concerto*

... rarely has so wretched a plant been rescued and nourished; rarely has so great a composer written such drivel. One has heard soldiers improvising showy and sentimental fantasies for canteen comrades, and making as good reach-me-down as Delius does write-me-down.

Professor Arthur Hutchings, *Delius*

## ANTONIN DVOŘÁK
*Requiem*

Dvořák's *Requiem* bored Birmingham so desperately that it was unanimously voted a work of extraordinary depth and impressiveness, which verdict I record with a hollow laugh, and allow the subject to drop by its own portentous weight.

George Bernard Shaw

## EDWARD ELGAR

The only composer who shows traces of his [Liszt's] influence is Elgar, and Elgar, despite his brilliant style is repugnant to many English musicians, by reason precisely of that chevaleresque rhetoric which badly covers up his intrinsic vulgarity.

Professor Edward J. Dent

# CÉSAR FRANCK

... an industrious schoolmaster and nothing more ... no invention nor any original impulses to drive him to invent.... nothing he wrote possesses any qualities beyond a certain mastery of technique ... and a certain perfectly individual clumsiness in applying that technique.

John F. Runciman, Saturday Review, May 1896

*Symphony in D Minor*

The affirmation of incompetence pushed to dogmatic lengths.

Charles Gounod

# GEORGE GERSHWIN
*Rhapsody in Blue*

How trite and feeble and conventional the tunes are, how sentimental and vapid the harmonic treatment, under its disguise of fussy and futile counterpoint.

Lawrence Gilman

It runs off into empty passage work and meaningless repetition.

Pitts Sanborn

# CHARLES FRANÇOIS GOUNOD
*Redemption*

... if you will only take the precaution to go in long enough after it commences and to come out long enough before it is over, you will not find it wearisome.

George Bernard Shaw

## EDWARD GRIEG
*Piano Concerto*

We cannot certainly say that definite themes are wanting ... but many of them are uncouth – the first especially ... and they appear thrown together, as if the composer had resolved to use up all the melodies he had jotted down at various times in his sketchbook.... the composition left a sense of weariness upon the audience.

*Musical Times* (1877)

*Scenes from Olav Trygvason*

The world has suffered many things through Grieg's experiments in the grand style of composition. I have no idea of the age at which Grieg perpetrated this tissue of puerilities; but if he was a day over 18 the exploit is beyond excuse.

George Bernard Shaw

*Violin Sonata* (Opus 13) and *String Quartet*

We have experienced nothing but distaste for the absurdities brought together under the cloak of nationalism, which scarcely conceals ... the insignificance of the invention, and above all the want of any power of organisation and development ... without letting the seams show.

*Signale*, November 1878

## FRANZ JOSEPH HAYDN

A mere fop ... a scribbler of songs.

Gregorius J. Werner (1695-1766)

## PAUL HINDEMITH
*Concerto for Horn, Brass and Strings*

For musical emotion there was now and then a wooden sigh, a metal tear, a fretwork laugh …

*Musical Times*, October 1927


*Overture 'News of The Day'*

Hindemith is the Hannen Swaffer of music; he has a facile technique that enables him to write about anything at any time with a superficial brilliance and pseudo profundity that are often taken for the real thing, as Butler put it: 'For daring nonsense seldom fails to hit, like scattered shot, and pass with some for wit.

*Musical Mirror*, October 1931


## ARTHUR HONEGGER
*Rugby*

Heaven knows that life, with its din and rattle and the hooting of motor horns, is sufficiently trying to the nerves without so called art being made subservient to the same end. Clever, you say? H'm yes, perhaps, but where's the inspiration?

*Musical Mirror*, October 1929


Expressions of contemporary life, fiddlesticks! … every musical layman that listens in to Savoy Hill regards these works as jolly good jokes, and nothing else. I, for one, don't blame them.

*Musical Mirror*, August 1931

ERNST KRENEK
*Piano Concerto*

... this music means nothing to the performers (even Viennese orchestral players admit it!), who therefore can only play the written notes mechanically without making sense of them. How much less sense must these notes make, then, to the innocent listener.

*Musical Times*, May 1938


GUSTAV MAHLER

All that high position, commercial and artistic propaganda, loyal friends and money, could do for his nine immense symphonies has been done; and yet they have long since ceased to count.

Dr Eaglefield Hull, *Musical Classical, Romantic and Modern*


*Second Symphony*

... a detailed annotation of what the music would be like if only the composer could think of the right notes ...

*Musical Times* (1931)


*Fourth Symphony*

... extremely disappointed. The material is very thin, and as regards orchestral *sound* Berlioz and Wagner have done it far more convincingly. It seemed to be an impertinence to want all those people to make that particular music, as if *size* had become a morbid obession with him.

John Barbirolli

## JULES MASSENET

... those who look a little below the surface find his music inexpressibly monotonous ... few of the real lovers of music will expect any of his works ... to keep their popularity after the death of the author.

Fuller Maitland, Grove's Dictionary of Music (1910)

## WOLFGANG AMADEUS MOZART
### *Quartet in D Minor*

... now that barbarians have begun to write music, we get passages that make us shudder. From two fragments of this new quartet we can decide that the composer (whom I do not know and do not want to know) is only a piano player with a depraved ear.

Anonymous contemporary critic

## ARTHUR NIKISCH

His interpretations were quite devoid of distinction. We have plenty of Conductors without a tithe of Mr Nikisch's reputation who could do as well as this.... Mr Nikisch has brought his *own* oboe player from Buda-Pest. Until we heard this gentleman we had no idea that so disagreeable a tone could be produced from the instrument.

Musical Times, June 1895

## IGNACZ PADEREWSKI

Regarded as an immensely spirited young harmonious blacksmith, who puts a concerto on the piano as upon an anvil, and hammers it out with an exuberant enjoyment of the swing and strength of the proceedings, Paderewski is at least exhilarating.... But his touch, light or heavy, is the touch that hurts; and the glory of his playing is the glory that attends murder on a large scale when impetuously done. Besides, the piano is not an instrument upon which you can safely let yourself go in this fashion.

George Bernard Shaw, *Music in London*, June 1890

## GIACOMO PUCCINI

*La Bohème*

If it will not perhaps greatly enhance his reputation, at any rate, it will not diminish it. The choice of the subject for operatic treatment can scarcely be considered a very happy one.

*Morning Post*, October 1897

*Madame Butterfly*

The dawn was good but the climax disappointing, Mrs Pinkerton was unnecessary and the two scenes of the last act struck one as being decidedly too much spun out. Signor Caruso sang so well that his appearance was easily forgiven but when he was not actually singing, some of the audience were moved to observe that he looked like the Inspector of Police in the first act.

*The Times*, December 1905

… whose strenuous strains and pathetic, not to say dismal story, appears to commend it to all tastes. Some sections of the audience may be inclined to steal out before the poor deserted creature commits *felo de se* …

*Musical Times*, July 1910

*Tosca*

The opera, the public is informed, has been produced with great success in … Italy and South America, and as far as I am concerned, the places are welcome to keep it.

*Morning Post*, December 1906

## SERGEI RACHMANINOFF
*First Symphony*

To us this music leaves an evil impression with its broken rhythms, obscurity and vagueness of form, meaningless repetition of the same short tricks, the nasal sound of the orchestra, the strained crash of the brass, and above all its sickly perverse harmonization and quasi-melodic outlines, the complete absence of simplicity and naturalness, the complete absence of themes.

*Anonymous contemporary critic (1917)*

*Piano Works*

… monotonous in texture … consists in essence mainly of artificial and gushing tunes and accompanied by a variety of figures derived from arpeggios.

*Grove's Dictionary of Music* (1923)

## ERIK SATIE
*Gymnopédies*

… sketchy, undeveloped and formless … All the idiosyncracies of mature 'impressionism's' vocabulary and syntax … does not seem to possess the composer's higher endowments.

*Musical Times*, December 1911

ARTHUR SCHNABEL

At my first recital I played a Schubert sonata.... one critic recommended I should apply for a position at the Institute for African Drum Languages (Trommelsprache).

*My Life and Music*

## ARNOLD SCHÖNBERG
*Five Orchestral Pieces*

The music resembled the wailings of a tortured soul, and suggested nothing so much as the disordered fancies of delirium or the fearsome, imaginary terrors of a highly nervous infant.

*Globe*, October 1912

They are formless, incoherent, disjointed and utterly defiant of all preconceived ideas of what constitutes music.... with the fourth number, the want of ideas and continued vagueness became wearisome, and this developed into absolute boredom in the Finale.

*Referee*, October 1912

Almost everybody present seemed bewildered, if not shocked.... most of the matter presented was ugly enough to suggest nothing but the distracting fancies of delirium.

*Musical Times*, October 1912

*Gurre-Leider* (first BBC performance)

The tonal mountain ... produced – I won't say a mouse, but a rabbit. The *Gurre-Leider* goes back on the shelf, the Schönberg bubble suffers a bad puncture, and the musical world may shake its head over the unwisdom of putting too many eggs – in this case about £2,000 I believe – into one basket.

*Musical Times*, March 1928

MT. SCHÖNBERG.

## FRANZ SCHUBERT

Perhaps a more overrated man never existed.... He has certainly written a few good songs, but what then? Has not every composer … written a few good songs? And out of the thousand and one with which Schubert deluged the musical world, it would indeed, be hard if some half-dozen were not tolerable. And when that is said, all is said that can justly be said of Schubert.

*Musical Times*, February 1897

The simple secret of the inadequacy of Schubert's piano writing in his sonatas, as compared with the full and finished work of Beethoven, is probably to be explained by his half-mastery of the instrument which Beethoven had completely subjugated to his will.

Edmoundstoune Duncan, *Schubert*

None but a virtuoso ever wrote with a full measure of success for the piano, and it is certain that Schubert fell short of that description.

Ibid.

*Symphony in C 'The Great'* (published 1840)

Then the symphony was put into rehearsal. Unfortunately, the members of the band laughed, it is said, at the triplets of the last movement.

Ibid. (At a subsequent rehearsal, in Paris, the orchestra refused to carry on beyond the first movement.)

## ROBERT SCHUMANN
*First Symphony* (British première 1854)

Incoherent and thoroughly uninteresting ... a dead failure and deserved it.

J.W. Davidson, *Musical World*

a piece of head work – robust in places, but in places, also very ugly ... [it will] never be wanted again.

Henry F. Chorley, *Athenaeum*

*Paradise and the Peri* (1856)

Robert Schumann has had his innings, and been bowled out – like Richard Wagner. *Paradise and the Peri* has gone to the tomb of the Lohengrins.

J.W. Davidson, *Musical World*

*Piano Concerto* (British première 1856)

... bristles throughout with the conceits and eccentricities which belong so disagreeably to the new school now struggling for existence in Germany, and of which Wagner and Schumann are the principal upholders and illustrators. It would be impossible to admire such oddities of thought and expression.

Anon.

## DMITRY SHOSTAKOVICH
*Seventh Symphony*

The only passage of outstanding character is a long ostinato on an incredibly commonplace tune of five notes.... the remainder of the seventy-five minutes is filled with quantities of uninteresting music too seldom relieved by clever contrivance or fine writing.

*Musical Times*, April 1942

JAN SIBELIUS
*Fourth Symphony* (second British performance)

We were informed in the analytical programme that the *Scherzo* is merry and buoyant, which causes one to wonder what sort of music Sibelius would write if he were depicting melancholy discontent.

*Musical Times*, May 1920


RICHARD STRAUSS
*Elektra*

He has the besetting Teutonic sin of over-statement, of being unable to see that the half is often greater than the whole; and all the blacking of his face and waving of his arms, and howling 'bolly-golly black-man – boo!' at us leaves us quite unmoved, except to smile and wish he wouldn't do it…. the theme of triumph in the finale is so cheap that it must have been picked up on the rubbish-heap of Italian or French opera.

Ernest Newman, *Testament of Music*


*Der Rosenkavalier*

A great deal of it is that vein of clever bluffing that Strauss has become far too addicted to of late. For a good hour and a half of the time he is simply chattering away without anything definite to say; with his harmonic cleverness and his consummate orchestral technique he can 'spoof' the unsuspecting listener into believing that something really musical is going on when it is not.

Ernest Newman, *Testament of Music*

*Salome* (US première)

On that occasion the critics went up into the attic and dusted off adjectives that hadn't been in use since Ibsen was first produced in London. I remember that 'bestial', 'fetid', 'slimy', and 'nauseous' were among the more complimentary terms....

Deems Taylor, Men and Music

*Till Eulenspiegel* (British première)

It may be shortly described as the most sensational and grotesque collection of organized noises as yet presented to a discriminative audience.... we refuse to accept this huge joke as an intelligible concert item. Those who have considered Berlioz's last movement of the *Fantastic Symphony* the wildest piece of music written, will not have to shift the balance on to the newer German writer.

*Musical News*, March 1896


*Domestic Symphony*

A cataclysm of domestic plumbing.

H.L. Mencken


One of the most embarrassing works in the history of music.
Wallace Brockway and Herbert Weinstock, *Men of Music*


... abject emptiness; I can't bring myself to discuss it temperately.
Alan Rich, *New York Herald Tribune*, October 1964

# IGOR STRAVINSKY

… he is entirely unable to formulate a musical idea of his own. As a member of a savage orchestra he might perhaps be allowed to play a recurrent rhythm upon a drum – as the only evidence of real form in his work is that kind of primitive repetition which birds and babies do very well … for he stands at the head of a movement which interprets much that is real and rotten in the modern world; he endeavours to disguise the rottenness, and leaves it the more desperate.

*Musical-Times*, June 1929

[his works show] … in an extreme form the commonest and most unmistakable symptoms of decadence – the fear and resultant atrophy of vital instincts.

'Philip Heseltine' (Peter Warlock)

*Symphony for Wind … In Memory of Debussy*

I had no idea Stravinsky disliked Debussy so much as this. If my own memories of a friend were as painful as Stravinsky's of Debussy seem to be, I would try to forget them. But perhaps it is not his heart, but only his art that is wrong … His music used to be original; now it is aboriginal.

*Musical Times*, July 1921

*Piano Concerto*

To try another description of the concerto, it is probably rather like Bach, as Bach seems to wireless listeners who hate the name Bach and want nothing but coon songs.

Richard Capell

The pleasure of seeing the composer of Petrouchka again was equalled only by the pain of hearing the composer of the piano concerto. It was sad to think that the one-time man of genius had degenerated into the manufacture of this ugly and feeble commonplace.

Ernest Newman

To the initiates or propagandists, it is no doubt a miracle of beauty, better than the Matthew Passion. The plain man would call it a hoax.

*Evening News*

*The Nightingale*

He might have achieved his object without so much unpleasant noise.

*Musical Times*, June 1914

*Le Sacre du Printemps* (first British concert performance)

Why, Mr Goossens, when I bought a seat for your concert last week, did you make me pay a guinea for a shilling's worth of music and twenty shillings' worth of noise?

George Bernard Shaw to Conductor Eugene Goossens

The music baffles verbal description. To say that much of it is hideous as sound is a mild description. There is certainly an impelling rhythm traceable. Practically it has no relation to music at all, as most of us understand the word.

*Musical Times*, June 1913

## Le Sacre du Printemps (French première)

One beautifully dressed lady in an orchestra box stood up and slapped the face of a young man who was hissing in the next box. Her escort arose, and cards were exchanged between the men.

Romola Pulsky, (later Nijinsky's wife)

Towards the end of the ballet, just before the beginning of the 'Sacrificial Dance', as the hitherto motionless figure of the Chosen Victim was seen to be seized by growing paroxysms of trembling, Marie Rambert heard the gallery call out, 'Un docteur ... un dentiste ... deux docteurs ...' and so on.

Eric Walter White, *Stravinsky: the Composer and His Works*

Diaghilev kept ordering the electricians to turn the houselights on or off, hoping in that way to quieten the audience. Nijinsky, with Stravinsky behind him, stood on a chair in the wings, beating out the rhythm with his fists and 'shouting numbers to the dancers, like a coxswain'. At the end of the performance everyone was completely exhausted.

Ibid.

## PETER TCHAIKOVSKY
### First Piano Concerto

Tchaikovsky's First Piano Concerto, like the first pancake, is a flop.

Nicolai Soloviev, *Novoye Vremya*, November 1875

To place Beethoven's *Symphony in A* and his *Violin Concerto* side by side with a rambling piece of musical incoherence, termed a Pianoforte Concerto by Tchaikovsky ... was scarcely a judicious proceeding ...

*Musical Times*, April 1877

### Fourth Symphony

The first movement is too long ... it gives the effect of a symphonic poem to which the composer has slapped on three more movements and called it a symphony ... There is one defect ... to which I shall never become reconciled; every movement contains places that remind one of ballet music.

Alexander Taneiev

### Sixth Symphony, 'Pathétique'

When the novelty of other music has worn off, a great part of it will be quickly shelved ... as time goes on ... There is pessimism and pessimism, of course; but the mere nervous worry of Tchaikovsky hardly deserves the name.

Ernest Newman, *A Musical Motley*

### Piano Trio in A Major

Tchaikovsky's *Piano Trio in A minor* was played in Vienna for the first time; the faces of the listeners almost expressed the wish that it should also be the last time.... It belongs to the category of suicidal compositions, which kill themselves by their merciless length.

Eduard Hanslick, *Am Ende des Jahrhunderts*

### RICHARD WAGNER

Wagner has good moments, but bad quarter-hours.

Gioacchino Rossini

I like Wagner's music better than anybody's. It is so loud that one can talk the whole time without people hearing what one says.

Oscar Wilde

*Siegfried*

... Siegfried seized some bits of a sword and sang: 'Heaho, heaho, hoho! Hoho, hoho, hoho, hoho! Heaho, haho, hahoo, hoho!' And that was the end of the first act. It was all so artificial and stupid that I had great difficulty in sitting it out. But my friends begged me to stay, and assured me that the second act would be better ... But the next scene ... was intolerable, with not the least trace of music in it ... With some courage I managed to wait for ... Siegfried's fight with the dragon.... but I could not stand it any longer; and I fled out of the theatre with a feeling of disgust that I have not yet forgotten.

Leo Tolstoy, *What is Art?*

*Lohengrin*

Richard Wagner is not a musician at all. Look at *Lohengrin* – that *best* piece; it is poison, rank poison. All we can make out of *Lohengrin* is an incoherent mass of rubbish with no more pretension to be called music than the jangling and clashing of gongs, and other uneuphonious instruments.

*Musical World* (1855)

Richard Wagner is a desperate charlatan – scarcely the most ordinary ballad-writer but would shame him in the creation of melody and no English harmonist of more than one year's growth could be found sufficiently without ears and education to pen such vile things.

Henry Smart, *Sunday Times* (1855)

*Tannhäuser Overture*

... one of the most curious pieces of patchwork ever passed off by self-delusion for a complete and significant creation. The instrumentation is ill-balanced, ineffective, thin and noisy.

H.F. Chorley, *Athenaeum* (1855)

A more inflated display of extravagance and noise has rarely been submitted to an audience.

*The Times* (1855)

### Die Meistersinger

If the 'Preislied' … be really a favourable specimen of Wagner's *Die Meistersinger*, we trust that our duty will not compel us to hear the rest of the Opera.

*Musical Times* (1870)

… Bayreuth … monstrous self-inflation … An earthquake would be good that would swallow up the spot and everyone on it.

G.A. Macfarren, Professor of Music
at the University of Cambridge (1876)

### Tristan and Isolde

Whether a drama treating of unrelieved tragic passion in a style of commensurate severity will ever gain the popularity of such works as *Lohengrin* or *Die Meistersinger* must appear doubtful.

*The Times*, January 1882

## CARL WEBER

Weber? His music gives me the colic.

Gioacchino Rossini

# PAINTERS & SCULPTORS

## CANALETTO (ANTONIO CANALE)

Canaletto, had he been a great painter, might have cast his reflection wherever he chose … But he is a little and a bad painter.

John Ruskin


## JEAN BAPTISTE CAMILLE COROT

The first impression of an Englishman, on looking at his works, is that they are the sketches of an amateur; it is difficult at first sight to consider them the serious performance of an artist...: I think his reputation … easily accounted for … Corot must be an early riser.

P.G. Hamerton


## DAVID COX and JOHN CONSTABLE

They represent a form of blunt and untrained faculty which in being very frank and simple, apparently powerful, and needing no thought, intelligence or trouble whatever to observe, and being wholly disorderly, slovenly and licentious, and therein meeting with instant sympathy from the disorderly public mind, now resentful of every trammel and ignorant of every law – these two men … represent in their intensity the qualities adverse to all accurate science or skill in landscape art: their work being the mere blundering of clever peasants …

John Ruskin

## GUSTAVE COURBET

... It is difficult to speak of Courbet without losing patience. Everything he touches becomes unpleasant.

P.G. Hamerton

## .GUSTAVE COURBET and JEAN FRANCOIS MILLET

... the painting of democrats – people who do not change their shirts and want to get the upper hand over decent society ... it disgusts me.

Count Nieuwerkerke

## CHARLES FRANÇOIS DAUBIGNY

If landscape can be satisfactorily painted without either drawing or colour – Daubigny is the man to do it.

P.G. Hamerton

## HILAIRE DEGAS

Degas is nothing but a peeping Tom. behind the coulisses. and among the dressing-rooms of the ballet dancers, noting only travesties of fallen debased womanhood. most disgusting and offensive.

*The Churchman*, May 1886

## JACOB EPSTEIN
*Strand Statues* (1908)

To the average man or woman … these figures will be occasions … for vulgarity and of unwholesome talk, calculated to lead to practices of which there are more than enough in the purlieus of the Strand already.

Father Vaughan, *Evening Standard*

… they are a form of statuary which no careful father would wish his daughter, or no discriminating young man, his fiancée to see … For a certain type of mind, on the other hand, it cannot but have a demoralizing tendency.

Ibid.

*Rima* (1925)

… stone-carving doesn't happen to be what he's best at … the stuff isn't flexible enough for him; he can't control it as he can clay … For the rest, his work is what you'd expect – dull, mechanical, lifeless – making the sculpture look as though Epstein had gnawed it with his teeth.

Eric Gill

Busts of *Anita* and *Mrs Epstein* (1926)

If these are Mr Epstein's best, then a poor artist would have done better if he had submitted his worst.

Lord Wavertree

*Night and Day* (1929)

... simplification which has degenerated into distortion and an expressionism which has ended in the grotesque ... the cult of ugliness seems to have taken the place of the search for beauty ... Bestiality still lurks below the surface of our civilization, but why grope about for it in the mud, why parade it in the open, why not leave it to wallow in its own primeval slime?

Sir Reginald Blomfield

*Genesis* (1931)

O you white foulness! ... He called you Genesis! ... this man who cracks bad jokes with a chisel ... The face is the face of a moron ... thick lips pout with a beastly complacence under the stone blob which I presume is the nose. Artistically, the thing is absurd. Anatomically, it is purely comic.

*Daily Express*


*Behold the Man* (1935)

We see only a distorted reminiscence of a man: the debased, sensuous, flat features of an Asiatic monstrosity.... it is ugly and vile.

*Catholic Times*


... an outrage, and I admire the *Daily Mirror* for refusing to publish a picture of the statue. It is one of the greatest insults to religion I have ever seen.

G.K. Chesterton


... he knows nothing about the man he has called Christ and portrayed ... I think he has done something outrageous.

Mary Borden


*Consummatum Est* (1937)

A disgusting travesty ... Artistically it is false ... Christ spent his life curing cripples. If he had seen Himself as Epstein has seen Him, He would have realized that there was not one piece of Himself that was not crippled. One cannot conceive of such a spirit inhabiting this gross and bloated form....

Sir Charles Allom

From the pictures it only looks to me like a child's first attempt with plasticine, the sort of unfortunate child who later gets looked at by a doctor and sent home.

*Universe*

All the necessary criticism of *Consummatum Est* is contained in the title. That is to say, Mr Epstein has used many hundredweights of alabaster to say a great deal less than is contained in two words....

*The Times*

Illustrations to *Les Fleurs du Mal* (1938)

... not only are they impertinent, they must be classed among the emptiest works that he has ever exhibited ... One does not need to be a Blimp in order to feel that ugliness is not enough....

*New Statesman*

Horror and near-obscenity, with no aesthetic value that I can perceive, stamp Epstein's new drawings ... The entire series – with misshapen females, sometimes decapitated, always repellent; lewd navvies fresh from, or leaving for, the torturer's rack; and disgusting embryos – is an insult to good taste – and to Baudelaire.

*Daily Mail*

PAUL GAUGUIN

I have just been skimming through an illustrated book called *Noa Noa* by a Frenchman, Paul Gauguin, which describes, or pretends to describe, a visit to Tahiti. Many of his figures are distorted, and all of them have a smutty look, as if they had been rubbed with lampblack or coal dust. When the Parisian becomes a degenerate, he is the worst degenerate of all – a refined, perfumed degenerate.

John Burroughs

## HOLMAN HUNT
*Light of The World*

A mere papistical fantasy ... empty make-believe ... a wilful blindness.

Thomas Carlyle

## THE IMPRESSIONIST SCHOOL

A period of ignorance and frenzy.

Hermann Bahr (1908: the first Impressionist
exhibition was given in Paris in 1874)

Here we can see that it is raining, we can see the sun is shining, but nowhere can we see painting.

Pablo Picasso

## AUGUSTUS JOHN

If only Augustus John had been serious what a fine painter he might have been.... in my opiniion 'the latest paintings' ... are almost worthless ... there is less talent than trick; and there is no thought at all.

Clive Bell, *New Statesman*, June 1938

## JOHN EVERETT MILLAIS
*Sir Isumbras at the Ford*

Not a fiasco but a catastrophe.

John Ruskin

*Christ in the Carpenter's Shop*

In the foreground ... is a hideous, wry-necked, blubbering red-haired boy in a nightgown, who appears to have received a poke in the hand from the stick of another boy ... and to be holding it up for the contemplation of a kneeling woman so horrible in her ugliness that ... she would stand out from the rest of the company as a monster in the vilest cabaret in France, or the lowest gin-shop in England.

Charles Dickens

CLAUDE MONET
First Impressionist Exhibition (Paris, 1874)

We are badgered enough with bogus eccentricity and it is only too easy to catch people's attention by doing something worse than anyone has dared to do it before.

Anonymous reviewer in *Charivari*

*Le Boulevard des Capucines*

Only, be so good as to tell me what those innumerable tongue lickings in the lower part of the picture represent?

Ibid.

*Impression Sunrise*

What does that canvas depict? Look at the catalogue ... 'Impression Sunrise.' Impression – I was certain of it. I was just telling myself that since I was impressed there had to be some impression in it....

Anon.

## HENRY MOORE

The statues are hideous beyond words, they seem to be a sort of primitive caveman production, and unworthy of a good place on any public building in London.

*Morning Post*, April 1929

I consider it an outrage to associate the words 'female figure' with such hideous lumps of stone as those recently depicted on the front page of your paper.

Surely the human form is the most beautiful of all beautiful things, and are we not told that God created man in His own image?

Letter to the *Daily Mirror*, April 1931

Sir, May I congratulate your Art Critic upon his excellent article entitled the 'Art' of Mr Moore, which appeared in Tuesday's issue?

It is splendid; he has hit the nail on the head, and covered the ground completely.

It is appalling to think that such influence is before the minds of those who will become teachers of sculpture in our Art Schools in the near future.

I trust that through the article attention may be drawn to the matter in Parliament.

Letter to The *Morning Post* April. 1931

Travel up to Northampton and see the statue of the madonna and child in this church. My horses may be all wrong; we all may be wrong; but I'm damned sure that isn't right.

Sir Alfred Munnings

## PABLO PICASSO

... if I met Picasso in the street I would kick him in the pants ... I find myself a president of a body of men who are what I call shilly-shallying. They feel that there is something in this so-called modern art.

Now we have all sorts of highbrows here tonight, experts who think they know more about art than the men who paint the pictures. They are – if I may use a common expression – so fed up to the teeth in pictures, they see so many pictures ... that their judgement becomes blunt, yes blunt! ... That reminds me of Anthony Blunt, is he here tonight? He once stood with me in this very room during an evening party when the King's pictures were here. There was a full-length Reynolds hanging on the end wall, a fine picture, and he was telling some people that Reynolds was not as good as Picasso. What an extraordinary thing for a man to say!

> Sir Alfred Munnings, in a televised speech after a dinner at the Royal Academy in 1949

They [Picasso and Gertrude Stein] are in my belief turning out the most Godalmighty rubbish that is to be found.

> Leo Stein, brother to Gertrude

*Guernica*

What we cannot forgive is the banality of overstatement, or the projection of irrelevancies into the foreground with the stamp of creative originality ... Picasso has failed to evoke the heroism of Guernica ... He has only substituted Gertrude Stein for Florence Nightingale.

> Francis Henry Taylor

*Still Life with a Bull's Head*

My little grand-daughter of six could do as well.

> Norman Rockwell

## THE POST-IMPRESSIONIST EXHIBITION
(Grafton Galleries, 1910)

An extremely bad joke or a swindle.

Wilfrid Blunt

Why talk of the sincerity of all this rubbish. Idleness and impotent stupidity, a pornographic show … the gross puerility which scrawls indecencies on the walls of a privy.

Charles Ricketts

This art stops where a child would begin … like anarchism in politics, it is a rejection of all that civilization has done, the good and the bad.

*The Times*

… all I could discover was a series of converging and retreating lines. Roger Fry the eminent critic … came up to me and said, 'Isn't there a wonderful expression on that woman's face?' I stared at Fry and I stared at the canvas; try as I would, I could see no expression, I could see no woman and I could see no face.

Alfred Sutro

## THE PRE-RAPHAELITES

Their ambition is an unhealthy thirst which seeks notoriety by means of mere conceit. Abruptness, singularity, uncouthness, are the counters by which they play the game.

Anon.

## RAPHAEL (RAFAELLO SANZIO)

The critic has actually imposed upon the world the superstition that a painting by Raphael is more valuable to the civilizations of the earth than is a chromo.

Mark Twain

## REMBRANDT (HARMENSZOON VAN RIJN)

Now it is evident that in Rembrandt's system, while the contrasts are not more right than with Veronese, the colours are all wrong from beginning to end.

John Ruskin

Vulgarity, dullness, or impiety will indeed always express themselves through art, in brown and grey, as in Rembrandt.

Ibid.

## PIERRE AUGUST RENOIR

Just try to explain to Monsieur Renoir that the torso of a woman is not a mass of decomposing flesh, its green and violent spots indicating the state of complete putrefaction of a corpse.

Albert Wolff (contemporary French art critic)

## AUGUSTE RODIN

Rodin set a very bad example to sculptors with his *Balzac*. He might have made either a portrait of Balzac or a symbol of his genius. As it was, he combined the two, and so queered the pitch of sculpture.

*Outlook*, February 1920

GRAHAM SUTHERLAND
*Portrait of Churchill*

How do they paint one today? Sitting on a lavatory! ... It makes
me look half-witted, which I ain't.

Sir Winston Churchill

... a striking example of modern art (laughter, applause) ...
Ibid., from the official record of his speech
at the presentation ceremony

If I had my way, I'd throw Mr Graham Sutherland into the Thames. The portrait is a complete disgrace … It is bad-mannered; it is a filthy colour … Churchill has not got all that ink on his face – not since he left Harrow at any rate.

Lord Hailsham

Portrait of Lord Beaverbrook

… looking very much like a diseased toad bottled in methylated spirit …

Quentin Bell

## HENRI DE TOULOUSE-LAUTREC

Among the painters of our period, Lautrec will certainly leave the trace of his curious and immoral talent, which was that of a deformed man, who saw ugliness in everything about him and exaggerated that ugliness, while recording all the blemishes, perversities and realities of life.

*L'Écho de Paris*, April 1899

The London Exhibition of May 1898

Really monstrous.

*The Star*

Revoltingly ugly.

*Lady's Pictorial*

He has but one idea in his head, and this is vulgarity.

*Daily Chronicle*

## JOSEPH MALLORD WILLIAM TURNER

This brown thing – is this your Turner?

Claude Monet

## DIEGO RODRÍGUEZ DE SILVA Y VELÁZQUEZ

Slovenly in execution poor in colour – being little but a combination of neutral greys and ugly in its forms.

*The Times*, June 1874

## PAUL VERONESE

Enter now the great room with the Veronese at the end of it, for which the painter (quite rightly) was summoned before the Inquisition of State.

John Ruskin, *Guide to Principal Pictures,*<br>*Academy of Fine Arts, Venice*

## JAMES ABBOTT MCNEILL WHISTLER

I have seen, and heard, much of Cockney impudence before now, but never expected to hear a coxcomb ask two hundred guineas for flinging a pot of paint in the public's face.

John Ruskin, *Fors Clavigera*, July 1877 (Whistler's<br>*Nocturnes* were exhibited in London in Spring 1878)

Nocturne, *The Falling Rocket*

This shows such wilful and headlong perversity that one is almost disposed to despair of an artist who, in a sane moment, could send such a daub to any exhibition.

*Daily Telegraph*

Nocturne, *Blue and Silver*

We protest against those foppish airs and affectations by which Mr Whistler impresses on us his contempt of public opinion.... It is very difficult to believe that Mr Whistler is not openly laughing at us.

*Pall Mall Gazette*

Nocturne, *Battersea Reach*

A few smears of colour, such as a painter might make in cleaning his paint brushes ... vaguely suggest a shore and bay.... One who found these pictures other than insults to his artistic sense could never be reached by reason.

*Knowledge*

Nocturne, *Cremorne Lights*

Some of the *Nocturnes* and some of the *Arrangements*, are defended only by a generous self-deception, when it is urged for them that they will be famous tomorrow because they are not famous today.

*Nineteenth Century*

*Arrangement in Silver and Black*

The artist has represented this bilious young lady as looking haughty in a dirty white dress ... and a grey hat with the most unhealthy green feather ... two dyspeptic butterflies hover wearily above her head in search of a bit of colour ... evidently losing heart at the grey expanse around.

*Society*

*Etchings of Venice* (1880)

They rather resemble vague first intentions, or memoranda for future use, than designs completely carried out. Probably every artist coming from Venice brings with him some such outlines as these in his sketch books. Apparently, so far as his twelve etchings are to be considered as evidence in the matter, Venice has not deeply stirred either Mr Whistler or his art.

*The World*

Another crop of Mr Whistler's little jokes.

*Truth*

So far removed from any accepted canons of art as to be beyond the understanding of an ordinary mortal.

*Observer*

We have seen a great many representations of Venetian skies, but never saw one before consisting of brown smoke with clots of ink in diagonal lines.

P.G. Hamerton

The series does not represent any Venice that we much care to remember; for who wants to remember the degradation of what has been noble, the foulness of what has been fair?

*The Times*

*Portrait of the Painter's Mother*

The picture has found few admirers ... and for this result the painter has only to thank himself.

*The Times*

# SCIENCE, TECHNOLOGY & INVENTIONS

## PLANETARY THEORY AND ASTRONOMY
*Galileo's Work*

… the theory that the Earth's movement is contrary to Scripture may neither be accepted nor defended … he must henceforth neither hold this theory, nor teach it, nor defend it, either orally nor in writing …

Cardinal Bellarmine

Animals, which move, have limbs and muscles; the earth has no limbs or muscles; therefore it does not move.

Scipio Chiaramanti

Buildings and the earth itself would fly off with such rapid motion that men would have to be provided with claws like cats to enable them to hold fast to the earth's surface.

Fromundus of Antwerp

The telescope does wonders upon the Earth, but represents celestial bodies falsely … reflected rays are the sole cause of Galileo's erroneous observations. I will never concede his four new planets to that Italian from Padua though I die for it.

Martin Horkey, English Astonomer

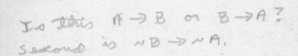

*The Discovery of Jupiter's Four Satellites* (1610)

There are seven windows in the head, two nostrils, two eyes, two ears, and a mouth; so in the heavens there are two favourable stars, two unpropitious, two luminaries, and Mercury alone undecided and indifferent. From which and many other similar phenomena of nature, such as the seven metals ... we gather that the number of planets is necessarily seven. Moreover the satellites are invisible ... can have no influence on the earth ... therefore do not exist.

Francesco Sizzi, Florentine astronomer

MEDICINE
*Anaesthesia*

We publish Herr Sertuerner's article [on his discovery of morphine] against our better judgement. It is highly unscientific and unchemical; if there is such a thing as Sertuerner's 'morphine' we chemists have much new to learn ...

Professor Ludwig Gilbert (1810)

The abolition of pain in surgery is a chimera. It is absurd to go on seeking it today. 'Knife' and 'pain' are two words that must *forever* be associated in the consciousness of the patient.

Alfred Velpeau, Surgeon (1832)

*Louis Pasteur's Discoveries*

It is absurd to think that germs causing fermentation and putrefaction came from the air; the atmosphere would have to be as thick as pea soup for that.

Dr Nicholas Joly of Toulouse (1840)

# ELECTRICITY
*Michael Faraday*

When Faraday showed proof of his discovery of electricity to Peel the Prime Minister, the Prime Minister asked him of what use it was – 'Who knows Sir,' Faraday replied, 'one day you might be able to tax it.'

## *Thomas Edison's Electric Light*

Do not bother to sell your Gas shares. The electric light has no future.

Professor John Henry Pepper

## *Nikola Tesla's Alternating-Current Electricity*

… high pressure, particularly if accompanied by rapid alterations, is not destined to assume any permanent position; it would be legislated out of existence in a very brief period even if it did not previously die a natural death.

Thomas Edison, pioneer of Direct-Current electricity

## *Electrical Power Supply*

I do not think the problem to transmit power by electricity from Niagara Falls to … varied distances up to 20 miles, a sound one commercially … if I were asked to invest any money in the enterprise, I would decline to do it.

Frank J. Sprague, electric railway pioneer

Trust you avoid gigantic mistake of adoption of alternating current.

Lord Kelvin, urgent cable to Edward Dean Adams<br>(President of the Niagara Falls Power Company)

TRANSPORT
*Railways*

Great improvements of the Age! What! to call the facilitation of death and murder an improvement! Who wants to travel so fast? My grandfather did not, and he was no fool ... snort! puff! scream! ... that iron fiend goes yelling through the land ... Would fifty conspiring mountains fall atop of him.

Herbert Melville

What can be more palpably absurd and ridiculous than the prospect held out of locomotives travelling *twice as fast as stage coaches*!

*Quarterly Review*, March, 1825

*The Motor Car*

There can be little doubt that the vast majority of people would prefer a smooth-running, reliable steam-engine ... to the evil-smelling dangerous, wasteful and at best uncertain and un-reliable [petrol] engine.

*Horseless Age*, February 1896

*Flight*

... artificial flight is impossible.

Simon Newcomb, Astronomer and Director
of the US Naval Observatory (1894)

... the first successful flying machine will be the handiwork of a watchmaker, and will carry nothing heavier than an insect. When this is constructed, we shall be able to see whether one a little larger is possible.

Professor Simon Newcomb, *McClure's*, September 1901

If such sensational and tremendously important experiments [the Wright brothers' flights] are being conducted in a not very remote part of the country ... is it possible to believe that the enterprising American reporter, who, it is well known, comes down the chimney when the door is locked in his face – even if he has to scale a fifteen-storey skyscraper to do so – would not have ascertained all about them and published them broadcast long ago?

*Scientific American*, January 1906

I confess that in 1901 I said to my brother Orville that man would not fly for fifty years ...

Wilbur Wright to the Aero Club of France, 5 November 1908

## The Submarine

At present, the German naval authorities have no high opinion of submarines as instruments of war. For the time being, however, they seem suitable for coastal defence, but will hardly ever be employable on the high seas.

Herr Victor Laverrenz (1908)

COMMUNICATIONS
*The Telephone* (patented in March 1876)

It is impossible to transmit speech electrically. The 'Telephone' is as mythical as the Unicorn.

> Professor Poggendorf (1860)

It's all humbug, such a discovery is physically impossible.

> Professor Tait on learning of Bell's invention

… while my partners and I enjoyed the demonstration of your invention, we have concluded that, although it is an interesting novelty, the telephone has no commercial application.

> J. Pierpoint Morgan, letter to Alexander Graham Bell

I fancy that the descriptions we get of its use in America are a little exaggerated; but there are conditions in America which necessitate the use of instruments of this kind more than here. Here we have a superabundance of messengers, errand boys, and things of that kind.

> Lord Lindsay to 1879 House of Commons
> Committee on Telephony

*Long Range Wireless Transmission*

If you could construct a mirror as large as a continent, you might succeed with such experiments, but it is impracticable to do anything with ordinary mirrors, as there would not be the least effect observable.

> Heinrich Hertz, discoverer of wireless waves

Signor Marconi's ingenious ideas do not seem to have made much headway.... The public will be well advised to keep clear of this concern.

New York investment broker's advice (1898)

*Television*

The most deeply rooted of my present opinions is that the future holds no place for the cathode-ray tube as a receiver for televised pictures ... My firm opinion is that some form of mechanical scanning must be used in the receiver unless we can get rid of scanning altogether. Both publicly and privately I have been attacked for this opinion, but no arguments have been advanced to cause me to abandon or even modify my conviction.

Captain Ernest Robinson, *Televiewing* (1935)

Improvements in television will not come by way of the cathode-ray tube. They will come by way of mechanical reproduction. I know, I travelled all over Europe last year and saw all their equipment, but I am still convinced that the cathode-ray tube does not hold the solution to the problem, that it lies in mechanical reproduction.

Dr Lee deForest, radio pioneer (1935)

I showed them my invention for a television. They evinced polite curiosity, then informed me that they were convinced that the transmission of images – especially mentioning fog as an impediment – was impossible.

J.L. Baird to Ronald Duncan (1940)

## ATOMIC POWER

Atomic Power is an illusion.

> Nikola Tesla inventor of the induction motor
> and pioneer of Alternating-Current electricity.

The energy produced by the breaking down of the atom is a very poor kind of thing. Anyone who expects a source of power from the transformation of these atoms is talking moonshine.

> Lord Rutherford, *Evening News*, September 1933

Rutherford shouldn't concentrate so exclusively on Nuclear Physics, because a great national laboratory should do things that were at least of some industrial significance.

> Professor Bragg (1938)

The fact is that, although we now know that matter can be converted into energy, we are aware of no greater prospect for destroying Nuclear matter for power purposes than of cooling the ocean … and extracting the heat for profitable work.

> Dr E.O. Lawrence, leading USA physicist (1938)

There is not the slightest prospect that this energy will ever be of practical use.

> Ernst Zimmer, *The Revolution in Physics* (1941)

That is the biggest fool thing we have ever done. The bomb will never go off, and I speak as an expert in explosives.

Admiral Leahy, US Navy, June 1945

## ROCKETS AND SPACE TRAVEL
*Rocket Propulsion*

With any car working on the principle of propulsion by means of a stream of escaping gases there must be someting substantial *behind* the car for the gaseous stream to react upon … In other words, a rocket car would have to be started from wall or from some other solid object in order that the gas stream *could impinge against it* and thus give the necessary push-off.

*Practical Mechanics*, September 1934

*Long Range Rockets*

… there has been a good deal said about a 3,000-mile high-angle rocket … such a thing is impossible and will be impossible for many years.… people have been talking about … a rocket shot from one continent to another carrying an atomic bomb, and so directed as to be a precise weapon which would land on a certain target … technically I don't think anybody in the world knows how to do such a thing and … it will not be done for a very long period of time to come … we can leave that out of our thinking.

Dr Vannevar Bush, Director of the Office for Scientific Research and Development, Washington, December 1945

… [a space] rocket will generate a red heat for the first hundred miles of its flight through the atmosphere … and vanish in an incandescent wisp of flame and smoke.

*Graphic*, November 1920

*Space Travel*

… in a sense interplanetary travel is and remains, utter bilge. It remains hideously expensive; the surface of the moon and planets are so inhospitable to life that there is no question of living on them; the difficulties of setting up a launching station to arrange a safe return are enormous …

Dr Richard Woolley, Astronomer Royal (1960)

... a stunt [which] if the world were a sane place would be dropped as quickly as possible.

*The Times*, April 1963

The Russians have come to the conclusion that it will be impossible for many years to come to get enough equipment on to the moon to enable a man to do a useful job of work and then get him back.

Sir Bernard Lovell, *Daily Mail*, July 1963

*Moon Landings*

... generations will pass before man ever lands on the Moon and ... there would be little chance of his succeeding in returning to Earth and telling us of his experiences.

Sir Harold Spencer Jones, FRS, *New Scientist*, August 1957